To: Lisa & Jeff

From: Lori + Scott

Happy Chennakah!
2006

Other books by Gregory E. Lang:

Why a Daughter Needs a Dad

Why a Son Needs a Dad

Why I Love Grandma

Why I Love Grandpa

Why a Son Needs a Mom

Why a Daughter Needs a Mom

Why I Chose You

Why I Love You

Why I Need You

WHY WE ARE A FAMILY

100 reasons

GREGORY E. LANG

CUMBERLAND HOUSE

NASHVILLE, TENNESSEE

WHY WE ARE A FAMILY
PUBLISHED BY CUMBERLAND HOUSE PUBLISHING, INC.
431 Harding Industrial Drive
Nashville, TN 37211

ISBN: 1-58182-468-8

Cover design: Unlikely Suburban Design
Text design: Lisa Taylor
Photographs and cover photo: Gregory E. Lang
Wedding photo: Lisa Davis

Printed in Canada
3 4 5 6 7 8 9 10— 11 10 09 08 07 06 05

To the sweet angels that always lift my heart—
Jill and Meagan Lang, and Linley Davis.

INTRODUCTION

I began this series of books on family relationships with a story about my family reunion, which takes place every Thanksgiving. I said that my family, now nearly seventy members strong, is the kind that embraces you, nurtures you, and loves you immeasurably. My family has been the bedrock of my life, understanding, accepting, loving, helping, and teaching me at every step along my journey. From my family I learned to put children first, respect elders, give care and solace to those in need, be thankful always, give and receive affection often, live up to your word and duty, forgive and let go, have fun, and never overlook a chance to tell someone "I love you." It is my family that I think about when in moments of reflection I ask myself what am I worth, what have I done with my life, and what am I going to do tomorrow? My family not only comforts me, they also give me meaning and purpose.

When I was young I would have told you that the definition of a family was a husband and wife and their natural-born children, all living under one roof. As I grew older and life events touched my family, I found reason to revise that definition. As divorce, death, or remarriage occurred, as enduring couples chose not to marry, I saw that merely being "intact" or having proximity and commonality did not define a family, and that the complexity of human relationships demanded a broader, more malleable, inclusive definition. I believe now that a family is not just the traditional two-parent variety that remains untouched by divorce, but also includes blended and single-parent families. These are indeed "families" because they share the same love, commitment, and concern that make a family what it is. I believe this because I have seen familial love extend beyond traditional family boundaries and legal arrangements, because I have felt the unmistakable gravitational pull that binds people together, the unconditional, unrelenting pull of the heart.

Although I boast of my family, it is in truth not unlike any other. We have been touched by death, divorce, disappointment, division, difficulty, and deception. We have secrets, conflict, and memories of broken promises. But we also have a rich history, treasured traditions, a theme of togetherness, a desire to embrace one another, a determination to overcome whatever separates us, and a will to welcome whomever wants to be among us. Yes, there are many examples of our fallibility, but there are many more of our love for one another and our lasting fellowship.

Perhaps the best example of what I describe about my family is illustrated in the following story. We were surprised one day a few years ago to learn that there was a new member of our family, someone who had been unknown to us for nearly twenty years. It was arranged for her to attend one of our gatherings, and on her arrival it was obvious to us all that she was one of us. Hours later, when all headed home, we left richer for including her in our family, and she went away with the knowledge that a bunch of once strangers were now a part of her family. Today we also count her husband and newborn child among us. It was this experience that taught me that you don't have to be born into a family to become a member of one, and that you don't have to earn the love and trust of family—it is yours without the asking.

In each book of this series I have focused on one of the relationships within a family—daughters and dads, sons and mothers, grandchildren and grandparents, and so on. In the course of writing these books and photographing those who shared their time and stories with me, I was struck by the love exchanged between the subjects of the particular book I was working on. But I was also struck by the palpable good feelings exchanged between everyone in the room who watched as I worked. Some of those watching were stepparents and stepchildren, others were adopted or foster children. None were of the opinion that they were not a family. All believed that what they shared was special, and all were proud to be the faces that would lend meaning to my words. By the end of my photo sessions it was more obvious to me than ever that my new definition of family was not unique to me—others shared it, lived it, and loved it.

While I initially intended to write about family relationships as a way to give thanks and recognition to those I love, I soon found the work caused me to be introspective. In many ways my books are confessional. I have shared with my readers that my only child is from a family divided by divorce. I have also shared that her mother and I have worked together, albeit not always easily, to give our child as much of a sense of family as we could given our circumstances. I have shared my fears, my regrets, some of my pain, and most of my hopes. What I haven't shared is my disappointment about not having the three children that I once hoped for, my concern that my daughter, Meagan, was missing something growing up as an only child, and my terrible loneliness in my empty house when she was spending time with her mother. These emotions sometimes kept me awake at night, brought tears to my eyes, or led me to pray for guidance and relief. Sometimes I would write about my feelings, hoping the exercise would give me an additional measure of strength to better carry my burden.

And then one day when I least expected it, God's grace rained down on me and my prayers were answered. Jill came into my life and brought with her a wonderful family of her own. Not only did I gain the benefit of falling in love and being loved in return, I gained a new extended family, one that welcomed me from the start and continues to extend sincere affection to me. I also gained the opportunity to have an important role in another young girl's life, to be a father figure to my wife's child, Linley. Meagan gained a stepsibling and the chance to know firsthand the love, fun, and trust that I share with all of my siblings. I now have a house that never seems to be empty. I wake up each morning happy to embrace my duties to these three women. I take great pleasure in readying the day for them and in the playful banter we share as each makes her morning appearance. I go to bed grateful that this blessing has come into my life, that I get to be both husband and father, that I have a family. That in *our* house, we have submitted to love's gravity, and it pulls us closer together, day after day.

WHY WE ARE A FAMILY

We are a family because

the well-being of each is important to all.

We are a family because

we are always happy to see one another.

We are a family because

we love to go places together.

We are a family because . . .

we can't stop telling those funny, embarrassing stories.

we take an interest in what is on one another's minds.

we don't require an apology before forgiving.

we create a little more history every day.

We are a family because

we believe that too much cannot
be asked of each other.

We are a family because

we can read each other's minds.

We are a family because . . .

we miss one another when we are apart.

we never fail to recognize each
other's accomplishments.

the strength of our bond is immeasurable.

others can just look at us and see that it is so.

We are a family because

we mindfully prepare for the future
of the little ones.

We are a family because

sometimes we want nothing more
than to relax together.

We are a family because . . .

we never hesitate to apologize to each other.

we love one another equally and unselfishly.

we honor our family traditions.

our hearts are lifted when we worship together.

We are a family because

we are always prepared to defend one another.

We are a family because

our sacrifices are made willingly.

We are a family because

even though we may be apart, we are always
together in our hearts and minds.

We are a family because

we know one another's weaknesses,
but we never exploit them.

We are a family because

our times together have been
the best times of our lives.

We are a family because

the evidence of our bond is everywhere.

We are a family because...

it never occurs to us that we shouldn't be together.

we are rich in love and compassion for all.

we hold one another up during times of sorrow.

we plan for the future—and the future includes everyone.

We are a family because

we do not hesitate to share our affections.

We are a family because

we consider the good for all
before the good for one.

We are a family because

we crave the comfort of our togetherness.

We are a family because

our faith binds us together.

We are a family because . . .

we embrace our duty to provide for those
who cannot do so for themselves.

none of us is ever more than a phone call away.

we would never willfully hurt one another.

our commitment to one another never
comes into question.

We are a family because

we help one another but we don't keep score.

We are a family because

we take the time to capture memories
of the special moments we share.

We are a family because

we respect each other's differences
and celebrate the things we have in common.

We are a family because . . .

we love to sit together and reminisce.

we enjoy sharing favorite family recipes.

we love to share the events of our day
with one another.

we can chat for hours and never get bored.

We are a family because

we don't violate the trust we have in each other.

We are a family because

we are stronger together than we are apart.

We are a family because . . .

we can always count on each other.

we never shy away from the hard choices.

we lean on one another for comfort and support.

we treat each other as equals.

We are a family because

we pull together to take care of the little ones.

We are a family because

we do not squander the time we have together.

We are a family because

we are the first to step in and protect each other.

We are a family because . . .

each of us is an irreplaceable part of the whole.

we pass down our family history.

we act as shepherds for one another.

without one another our lives would be
less than what they have become.

We are a family because

there's a little bit of each of us in all of us.

We are a family because

we celebrate with abandon when we get together.

We are a family because

we sing "Happy Birthday" to the young and old alike.

We are a family because

we never fail to give a warm hug
when someone reaches out.

We are a family because

we make sure that everyone has a turn
to choose what we will play.

We are a family because

there can be no other explanation for how much
we love each other.

We are a family because . . .

we have always overcome our challenges.

we know when to laugh at one another
and when to give comfort.

together we are building a foundation
on which others will grow.

we save and pass on our most treasured keepsakes.

We are a family because

we always forget after we have forgiven.

We are a family because

nothing is more important to us
than being together.

We are a family because

we are thrilled when a newcomer is on the way.

We are a family because . . .

we wouldn't think of not spending the holidays together.

we make a place at the table for everyone.

we respect each other's privacy but permit
no one's isolation.

each of us resists any temptation that could harm all of us.

We are a family because

we are one another's biggest fan.

We are a family because

we look to each other for guidance.

We are a family because

in times of need, we never hesitate
to pull together.

We are a family because...

our membership is not conditional
and need not be renewed.

we remember and honor all of us—
even when they are not with us.

we believe there are no secrets that must be kept.

we never close the door on each other.

We are a family because

we never let life get so busy that we lose touch
with each other.

We are a family because . . .

we have a secret language.

we understand things that others just don't get.

no matter where we are, we always know where home is.

we have the concern and the will
to confront each other when necessary.

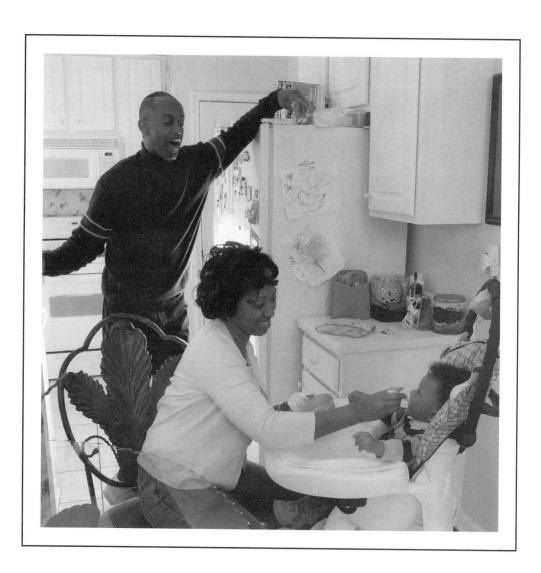

We are a family because

we enjoy beginning each day together.

We are a family because

we are teachers for one another
in the lessons of life.

We are a family because

we embrace each other's wild and crazy ways.

We are a family because . . .

it doesn't matter why any one of us might have left,
they are always welcomed back.

we honor our elders and the sacrifices they
have made on our behalf.

whatever one of us has to say is always
interesting to someone.

we are willing to do the hard work that benefits us all.

We are a family because

we choose to share our hearts with one another.

We are a family because...

we provide a safe harbor for any one of us that needs it.

we courageously overcome our disappointments and
patiently await new opportunities.

we always receive from one another more
than we have asked for.

we have the resolve to strive to improve ourselves
so that we may give more to one another.

We are a family because

when we are afraid, we give each other reassurance.

We are a family because

the love between us continues to grow.

Acknowledgments

I owe a heartfelt thanks to many—to Ron Pitkin, my publisher, who has given me a venue for saying the kinds of things that most of us regret not having said, and the staff at Cumberland House, including my editor, Lisa Taylor, who has made a welcomed imprint on all the books of the Why series; to everyone who is a part of the Obie Lee and Annie Ruth Brown extended family; to my parents, Gene and Dianne Lang, for every sacrifice you made on my behalf; to Johnny and JoAnn Parris, for welcoming me into your family; and finally to those that make my house a home: Jill, my wife and best friend, and Meagan and Linley, who all together promise to keep me on my toes for years to come.

To Contact the Author

write in care of the publisher:
Cumberland House Publishing
431 Harding Industrial Drive
Nashville, TN 37211

or e-mail the author:
greg.lang@mindspring.com